WHITEBOARD

WHITEBOARD

Business MODELS
That INSPIRE
ACTION

Daren Martin, PhD

Clovercroft Publishing

Whiteboard: Business Models That Inspire Action

Brown Books Publishing Group
16250 Knoll Trail, Suite 205
Dallas, Texas 75248 ← amazing city
www.BrownBooks.com
(972) 381-0009

A New Era in Publishing®

ISBN 978-1-61254-860-9
Library of Congress Control Number 2015943712

Printed in the United States
10 9 8 7 6 5 4 3 2 1 (Blast off!)

For more information or to contact the author, please go to...
www.WhiteboardModels.com

⤴ Legal Stuff

Dedicated to...

Jordan Martin
Madison Martin
Callahan Martin

You are my joy
and inspiration!

"Scratch the surface
in a typical boardroom and
we're all just cavemen
with briefcases hungry for
a wise person to tell us stories."

—Alan Kay

THIS BOOK

Quotes, pictures, diagrams and business models are all "stories" that communicate reality, jar thinking, disrupt the status quo, spark ideas, and drive change.

This collection of thought stirrers is drawn from things I have used over the years to initiate significant conversations and drive change at companies.

Use this book for personal inspiration or as a powerful management tool.

CULTIVATE

CULTIVATE CULTURE

Great companies and cultures do not happen by accident. They have to be cultivated.

Castle or Silo Organizations

When parts or all of your organization operate as little fiefdoms with no understanding of or regard for the total enterprise... your efficiency, effectiveness, and profitability are crippled!

Body Organizations

These organizations have integrated parts that thrive on their interdependence. Each part understands its role in the larger enterprise. They are more efficient, effective, and profitable!

Castle Organization

Body Organization

15

From the top of an organization, you can see far but only a few levels deep into the organization.

From the bottom of an organization, you cannot see the 20,000 foot view and only a few levels up.

Successful organizations find ways to communicate up and down the mountain!

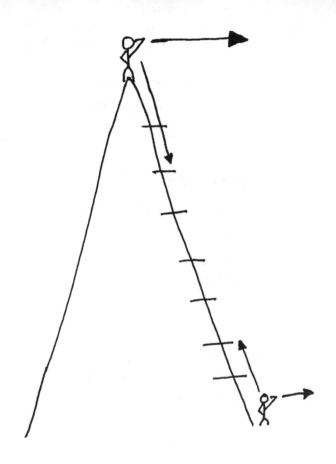

Organization
Perspective

The "Small" Stuff
MATTERS

Inefficiencies

Work arounds; fixes not
solutions, out dated
methods, no standard
process

Disrepair

Broken or outdated
equipment, shabby
work areas

Poor Performance

Low performers, bad
attitudes, no empower-
ment, bureaucracy

Broken Window
Theory of Crime

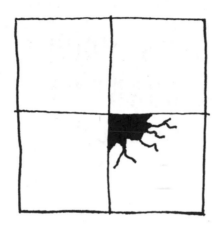

Principle: If a broken window
is left unattended,
Crime increases in
that area.

Why? People assume no
one cares about
that area so they
can do whatever.

IS YOUR
CURRENT
CULTURE

scALABLE?

"You can't put

$10 million in a
$5 million business

(You have to expand)."

— Michael Carrigan

If team members are misusing the internet, address it directly rather than limiting everyone's access.

Don't use an IT
Solution to solve a
personnel problem!

Many companies have a significant gap between their stated culture (the one posted in the lobby) and their hidden culture (the reality of what's really going on).

MIND
THE
GAP!

Stated Culture

Hidden Culture

HIRE the right people for a job
TRUST them to do that job
GIVE them the resources they need

(Without them having to play
games or trick the system!)

If you want a
ask for a ?

Much better
to build a culture where...

If you need a
ask for it and get it!

Worst: You need a
but ask for a !

Clunky processes
kill productivity!

Which Reflects Your Process?

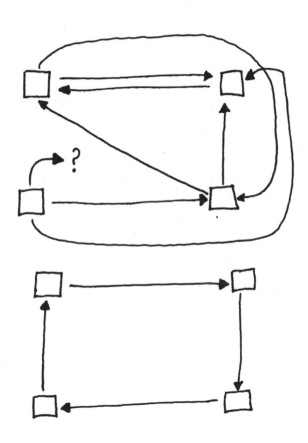

What are your
company's weak
links?

You are only as
strong as the weakest
Link.

MOVE...

Decision Making

Empowerment

Resource Access

Direction

CLOSER TO
THE VALVE

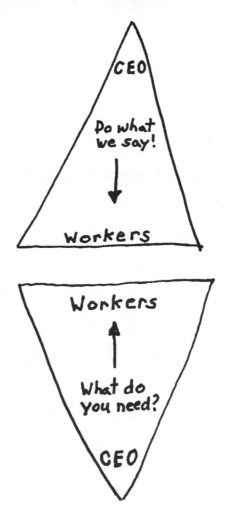

Your employees come first.
And if you treat your employees
right, guess what? Your customers come back and that
makes your shareholders
happy. Start with employees
and the rest follows from that.

—Herb Kelleher

What's the difference...

vs.

vs.

(nurture)

Does your company produce . . .

HIGH JUMPERS or...

CEILING BUMPERS ?

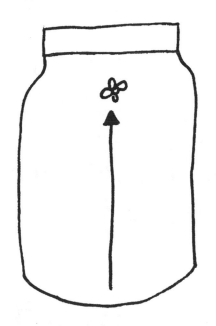

Leave a flea in a 14 inch jar, and when released, he will only jump 14 inches (even though he was capable of much higher)!

Do your employees
have ideas?

What happens to them?

What Is Your Philosophy?

"Why when I ask for
a pair of hands do
I get a brain?"
                    -Henry Ford

↰ vs. ↳
        ↓

Toyota gets an
average of 40
ideas a year from
every employee.

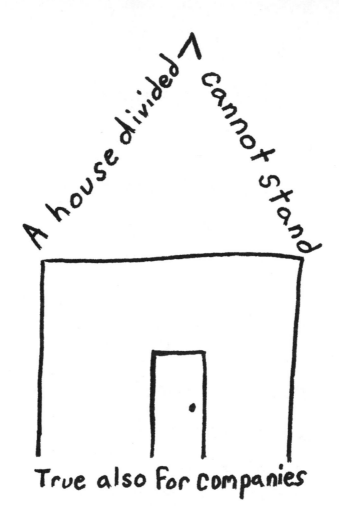

A house divided cannot stand

True also for companies

You cannot build a
nation (or company)
under 1,000 Flags.

Eliminate poison from your organization or Company!

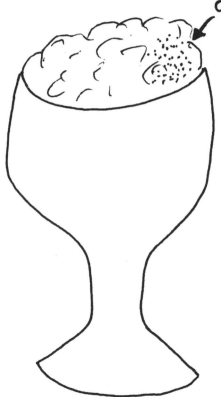

Remove barriers and bottlenecks!

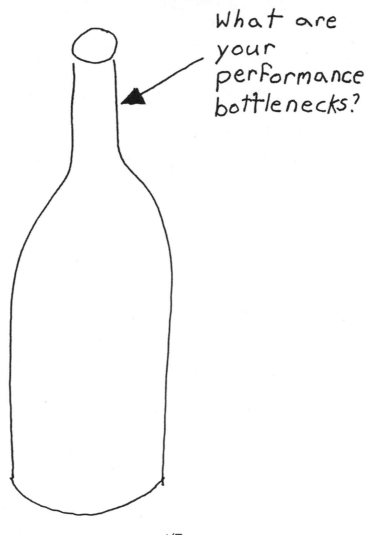

CHANGE

"The only way to change is you have to CHANGE."

I came up with this silly but true maxim. Mastering change is vital to success.

If you are not heading
in the right direction...

CHANGE DIRECTION

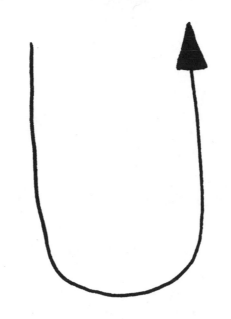

ALL U TURNS...
are legal!

If you are NOT reinventing your business, you are DOOMED!

"Pursuing incremental improvements while rivals reinvent the industry is like fiddling while Rome burns!" - Gary Hamel

My Favorite Model

CHANGE

Best place to change. Resources and momentum. Hard to convince people!

Hardest place to change. No resources. Easy to convince people!

COMMUNICATE

Don't just communicate how great it will be when we get here!

Also communicate it may be worse before it gets better!

COMPANIES

Sears
Enron
Blockbuster

IBM
McDonalds
Apple
Walmart

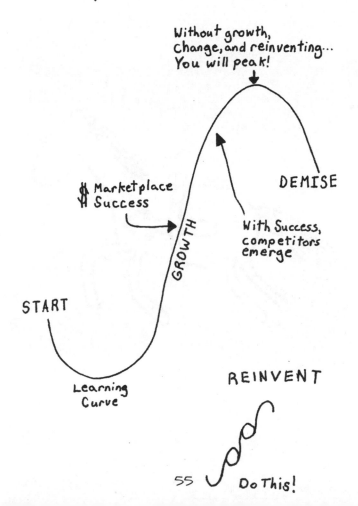

"If I'd listened to customers, I'd have given them a faster horse."

– Henry Ford

NEVER do it the hard way when more impactful and easier solutions are available!

Where do you start
to clear a log jam?

Here?
(front)

or Here?
(back)

Big Circle things include...

Weather
Economy
Laws
Global Unrest
Other People

Inner Circle things include...

Planning
Spending and Saving
Voting
Being Informed
Your Attitude

1. Mistake #1

Focusing on or worrying about things over which you have no control!

2. Mistake #2

Shrinking your actual circle of control and believing you have less ability to impact change than you actually do!

CIRCLE of CONTROL

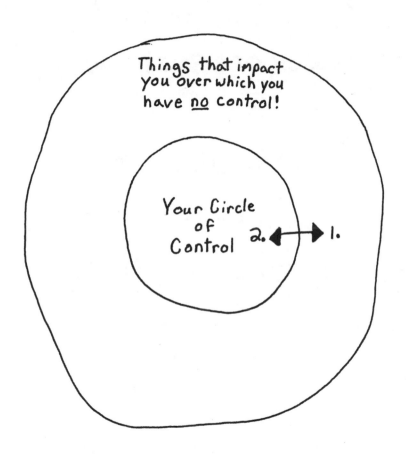

Things that impact you over which you have **no** control!

Your Circle of Control

2. ⟷ 1.

Many company ill-
nesses are systemic.

Heal the disease
rather than
masking symptoms

Ⓞ Aspirin ⟶ Immediate

Ⓞ Antibiotic ⟶ Process

Most organizational change
functions as an antibiotic with
progress not being immediately
observable. Give it time
to work.

Bonus

When you can provide

ALL 3!

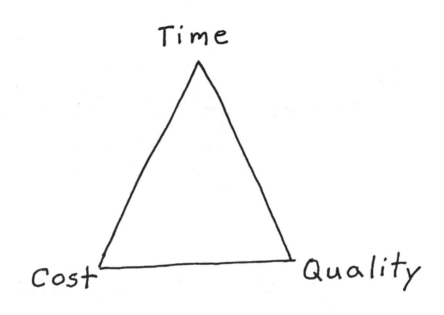

Which 2 do
you want?

One of the most valuable models available for mapping a plan!

I have used this model in <u>many</u> Strategy Sessions!

GAP ANALYSIS

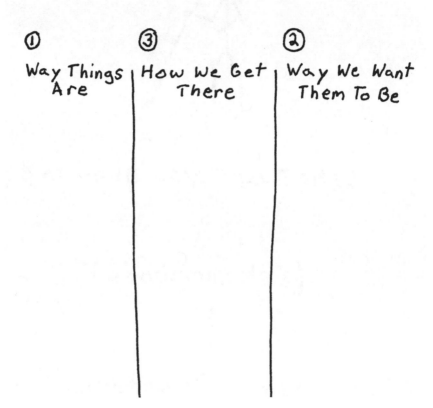

① Way Things Are

③ How We Get There

② Way We Want Them To Be

What are you blind to?

(ask somebody)

and listen

JOHARI WINDOW

	Known by Self	Unknown by Self
Known by Others		
Unknown by Others		

(What you DON'T know CAN hurt you!)

Fresh eyes yield
Fresh insights!

"Fish discover water last!"

— French Proverb

LEAD

LEAD don't follow.

Every company and country needs leaders. What kind of leader are you?

An army of

led by a

will defeat an army of led by a

— Genghis Khan

Which one
LEADS
at your
COMPANY?

Is your leadership the GOLD standard

or...

FOOL'S gold ?

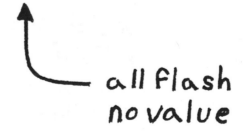 all flash no value

"If the Gold rusts,
what will the Iron do?"

– Canterbury Tales

SOFT SKILLS
are the
HARD SKILLS

(That pay dividends)

"The ability to deal with people is as purchasable a commodity as sugar or coffee and I will pay more for it than for any other commodity under the sun!"

— John D. Rockefeller

Every time you effect change, advance an agenda, or use others to accomplish a task, you either expand your influence with others or you shrink it depending on how you go about it.

Influence

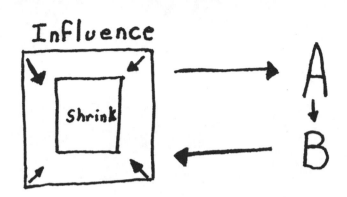

How you get things done either
Shrinks or expands your
influence.

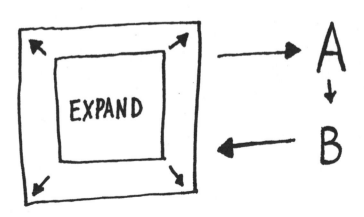

Which prevails at your company?

Management Styles

Abusive
Parent

Negligent
Parent

Collaborative
Pa~~re~~nt
Partner

SUBSTANCE

VS

 SMOKE and Mirrors

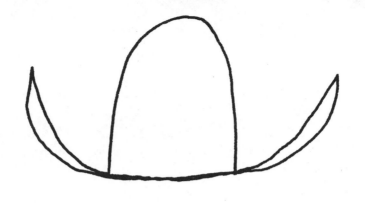

"All hat
no cattle."

—Texas Expression

COMMUNICATE
fully and accurately!

When making BIG changes, be decisive and thorough, not tentative and incremental.

Think pulling off a Band-Aid.

"If you are going to
cut the tail off
the dog, DON'T do
it one inch at a time!"

– Unknown

Employees...

Do what they are told... nothing more
Punch a clock
Take no ownership
Are fine with status quo
Gripe about problems

Owners...

Do what is needed... and more
Work to advance the company
Act like it is their company
Question status quo
Develop Solutions

Hint: We are talking about attitude
and action... not whose name
is on the deed!

FIRE Employees!

HIRE Owners!

Jerks take a
toll on morale and
performance.

↑
└ is it worth it?

Mean People Suck!

$$\left(\begin{array}{c} \text{The life out of your} \\ \text{COMPANY} \end{array} \right)$$

Question: Given a choice, would you pick Person B or Person C ?

Why ?

Talent Evaluation

	Skill		Attitude		Performance
Person A	10	x	10	=	100
Person B	10	x	4	=	40
Person C	4	x	10	=	40

Skill: Technical, knowledge, expertise, ability

Attitude: Leadership, positive, team builder, influencer, innovator, invested

Scale

1 ————————————— 10

Poor   Stellar

+ + = Rockstar

+ − = Eroder

− + = Pleaser

− − = ??? Why are they there?

Performance Management

Results You Get	How You Get Them
+	+
+	−
−	+
−	−

Be a "++" manager!

I drew the top
one for a manager
who asked me to
evaluate his meeting.

I told him I would
be exhausted!

Meetings

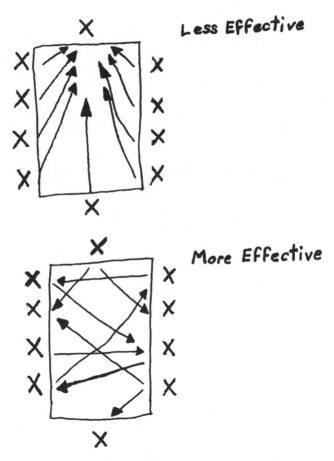

Less Effective

More Effective

Is your company producing LEADERS or followers?

"Effective LEADERS
are made not born."

– Colin Powell

Don't cram

SQUARE pegs

in ROUND holes!

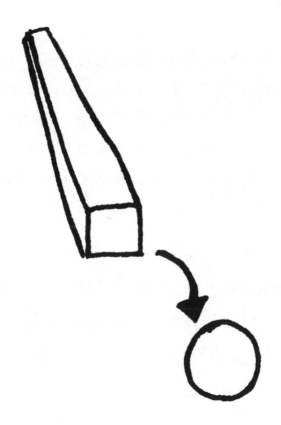

Use this feedback tool on a regular basis. Share one of each (start, stop, continue) with a boss, co-worker, or employee and ask for the same in return.

*Remember – it may start with surface stuff, but it will grow in value if you **stick** with it!

START · STOP · CONTINUE

START
(What I want you to start doing!)

STOP
(What I want you to stop doing!)

CONTINUE
(What I want you to continue doing!)

Smarter than everybody

Read nothing

Pontificate

Are always right

Scoff at new ideas

T
A
L   never listen
K

Beware the person who is always the TEACHER never the STUDENT!

METHOD 1

Provides too much freedom on the front end. Have to tighten expectations when things don't go well.

METHOD 2

More limited freedom at first that expands with performance.

COMMUNICATING
EXPECTATIONS

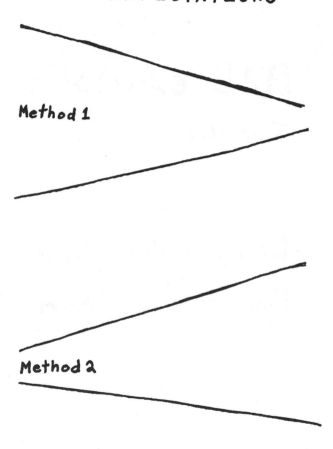

Method 1

Method 2

BAD examples
abound

Don't follow them
Don't hire them

Leading by example
is a bad thing if you are
a bad example!

COMMUNICATE

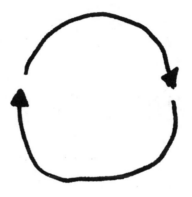

Companies that COMMUNICATE well consistently outperform companies that communicate poorly.

Who are your

(are you leveraging them?)

COMMUNICATION

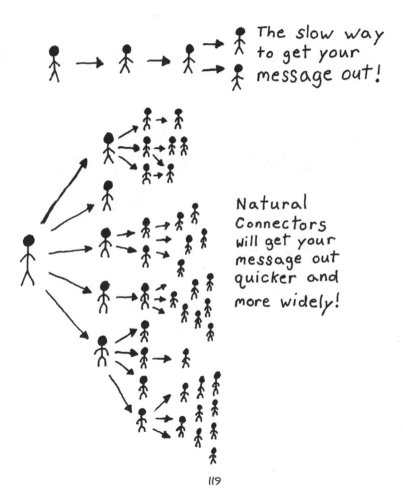

The slow way to get your message out!

Natural Connectors will get your message out quicker and more widely!

Generally, achievement is more valued than handouts.

Cat String Theory

A vision is mean-
ingless unless others
see it.

Just because you get it
doesn't mean others do!

5 LEVELS

of Vision Acceptance

1. Doesn't understand the vision- rejects the vision

2. Understands the vision - rejects the vision

3. Doesn't understand the vision- accepts the vision

4. Understands the vision- accepts the vision

5. Understands the vision, accepts the vision, AND... Contributes value to the vision

What's BIG to you
may be small to everyone
else!

My Issue

Seek First to
UNDERSTAND,
then to be
UNDERSTOOD.

— Stephen Covey

The wise person
listens before
speaking.

Learn THIS and nothing else and you will be crazy SUCCESSFUL!

"If there is any one
secret of success,
it lies in the ability
to get the other
person's point of
view and see things
from that person's
angle as well as from
your own."

— Henry Ford

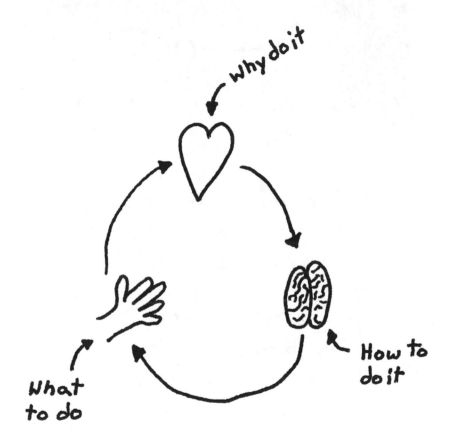

Why do it

How to do it

What to do

ENGAGE

 Do they care?

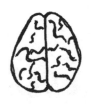 Do they understand?

 Do they act?

Words are
CURRENCY

— Tammy Kling

ACTions establish
the value of your
currency!

BUILD bridges
ELIMINATE tunnels
VALUE transparency

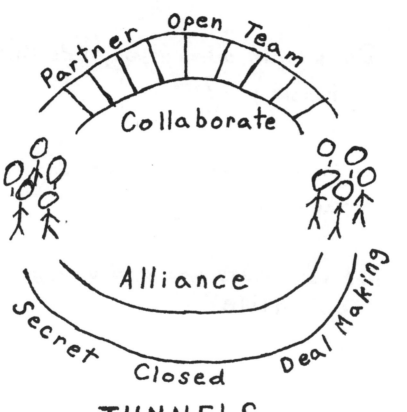

Do people admire you, or do they follow you?

Do your words amaze, or do they inspire?

Are your messages and words actionable?

When Cicero spoke,
the crowds declared,
"How well he spoke."

When Demosthenes spoke,
the crowds declared,
"LET US MARCH!"

Step by Step

Good when building or assembling. Not good when variations may occur.

Objective Focused

Good when you don't want barriers to derail from the final objective.

Marching Orders

Step by Step

1. Go to the town Bippel. → 2. Meet Ned; he can provide shelter.

3. Move on to Mdano. Dani can provide explosives. → 4. Go to the Zing bridge - blow it up!

Objective Focused

Objective: Blow up the Bridge!

Potential Resources: Ned in Bippel, Dani in Mdano

NO   Spin

NO   Whitewash

NO   Cover-up

NO   Minimizing

NO   Smoke and Mirrors

Call it what it is!

"The beginning of WISDOM is calling things by the right name!"

— Chinese Proverb

Solution-Focused Negotiating

1. Focus on what you agree on!

2. Take time to understand what the other party wants and why.

3. Look for solutions that give both parties what they want.

4. Treat the other party with respect.

Negotiating Success

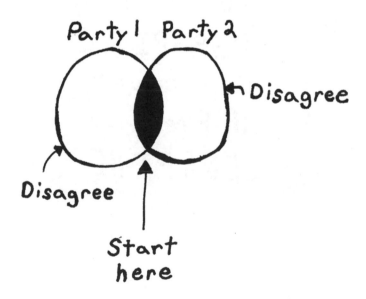

People will
PERSPIRE
for a cause
if first you
INSPIRE

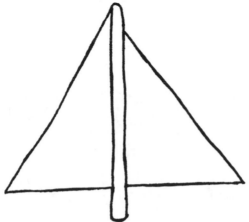

"If you want to build a ship
don't drum up people to
collect wood and don't
assign them tasks and
work, but rather teach
them to long for the
endless immensity of the sea!"

– Antoine de Saint-Exupéry

Being able to explain
Complex ideas in an
understandable way
is a valuable skill.

"YOU do not really understand something UNLESS you can explain it to your grandmother!"

-Albert Einstein

How we think things work

$$A \longrightarrow C$$

In reality

$$A \rightarrow B \rightarrow C$$

Chris walks by and does not say "hi"

I conclude he is rude

I leave him off a group lunch invite

(Reality: Chris was pre-occupied with news about a friend's death!)

A = An event occurs

B = We apply an interpretive grid to the event which may or may not be accurate

C = We have an emotional and behavioral response

ASK, don't ASSUME!

GROW

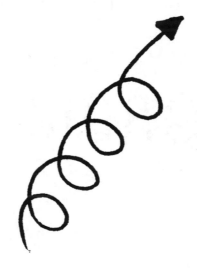

Grow or die!
If you are not
growing, you
are dying!

Experiment

Kindergarteners were
asked what they saw.
They had a variety
of answers – "smashed
bug" etc.

High School students
said, "a black dot
on the board!"

What
do you
See?

If all you see is a black dot,
you need to boost
your creative vision!

Occam's Razor

Of two competing theories or explanations, all other things being equal, the simpler one is to be preferred.

—William of Ockham

In London, if you
hear hoofbeats outside...

Think  (horse)

Not  (zebra)

Whether you think
you CAN or think
you CAN'T you
are RIGHT.

— Henry Ford

"Argue for your limitations and sure enough, they're yours!"
-Richard Bach

Bonus leader points for

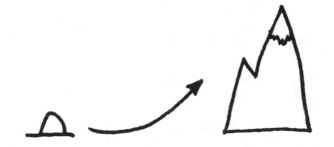

catching molehills that
are growing into mountains.

Problem: Making
a mountain out
of a molehill.

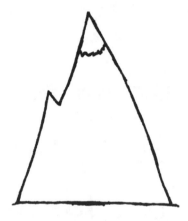

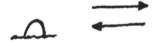

Bigger Problem:
Viewing a mountain
as *simply* a molehill.

Bring a well-thought-out plan. Not just an idea.

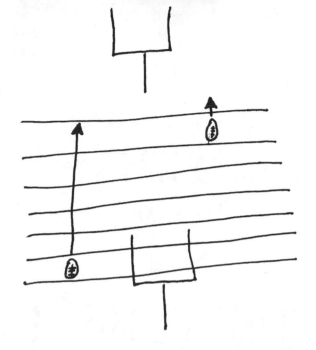

Plans are more often approved when delivered on the 10 yard line than with 90 yards to go.

Don't
shrink
the
UNIVERSE!

Scarcity Mentality

Abundance Mentality

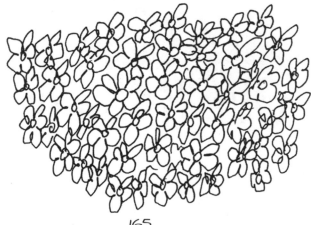

UNDER Promise

OVER Deliver

Promise this

Deliver this

Technical Skills
may get you a job

Vision
Creative
Leadership
SKILLS
Team
Communication
People

Will get you a career

What Matters As You Advance

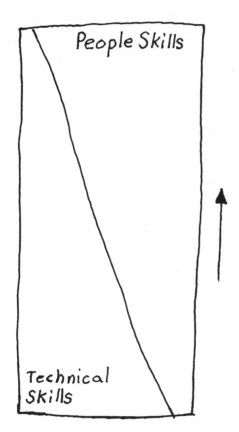

Most skills worth
having are forged
from persistence.

Don't be like the guy who said, "I tried playing the piano once, but it didn't work!"

There is way
more to the

than you are
choosing to see!

Your Vision
is influenced by...

Mood

Training

Fears

Wants

Beliefs

Past

Biases

Preference

Dreams

Culture

Others

Experiences

Perspective

In Business
and life
you

REAP

what you

SOW

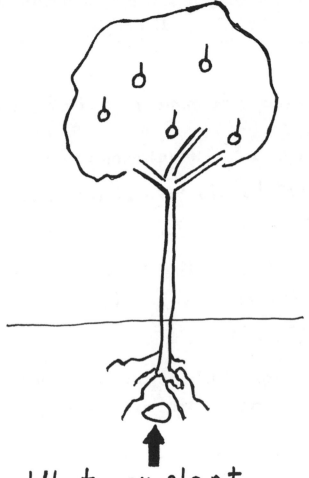

What you plant
is what grows.

Great Goals

- Read like miniature short stories.

- Are written in paragraph (not bullet) format and are 1-5 sentences.

- Don't bury the lead! Start with the value the goal provides.

- Assign metrics to words like increase, decrease, improve...

- Answer the "so what?" or "why is this worth doing?" question.

Anatomy of a Goal

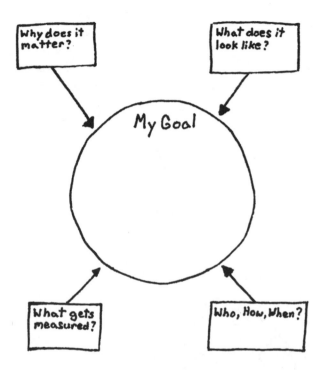

"In the absence of clearly defined goals,
we become strangely loyal to performing
daily trivia until ultimately we become
enslaved by it."

– Robert Heinlein

"This nation, before this decade is out, will land a man on the moon and return him safely to Earth!"

— John F. Kennedy

This goal inspired and organized an entire nation around a desired objective.

Do <u>You</u> Focus On...

Assets	Liabilities
Solutions	Barriers
Possibilities	Limitations
Abundance	Scarcity

or

?

The Proverbial Glass Question

$\frac{1}{2}$ empty

$\frac{1}{2}$ Full

For some people, not only is the glass half empty in their mind, it's also poisoned!

Do ideas thrive
at your company
or perish?

INNOVATION

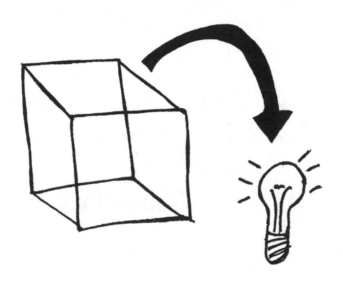

The best way to come up with a great idea is to have lots of ideas!

"The only thing I know for sure is that I know nothing!"

— Socrates

! = Ignorance

? = Wisdom

$$\left(\begin{array}{l}\text{Questions lead to} \\ \text{richer, more complete} \\ \text{strategies.}\end{array}\right)$$

To lead without a title
is to derive your power
within the organization
not from your position but
from your COMPETENCE,
effectiveness, relationships,
excellence, innovation,
and ethics.

— Robin Sharma

LEVELS of COMPETENCE

Consciously
Competent — (Can do it and teach others)

↑

Unconsciously
Competent — (Can do it but not sure how)

↑

Consciously
Incompetent — (I know what I don't know)

↑

Unconsciously
Incompetent — (Dangerous)

Are you a...

$+$ $\times$

or a ...

$-$ $\div$

(Be a (x) multiplier)

ADDitude

Your attitude
either adds or
subtracts!

Take classes
Read a book
Find a Mentor
Add new tools
Take a break
Meditate
Explore Something
Improve process

To save time
chopping down a
tree, spend
time sharpening
your blade.

Take your best and **1%** it! Slight changes and improvements can yield big results!

Don't just look for big shifts. Keep tweaking and improving!

The Bridge
Falling Down

Water
or
Steam

Making the Turn
or
Hitting the Wall

Landing
or
Crashing

Life
or
Death

1°

Gold Medal
or
Silver Medal

DIFFERENCE

Water
or
Ice

Millions
of $

Home Run
or
Out

Made Free Throw
or
Missed Free Throw

COLLABORATION

is

KING

MANAGEMENT

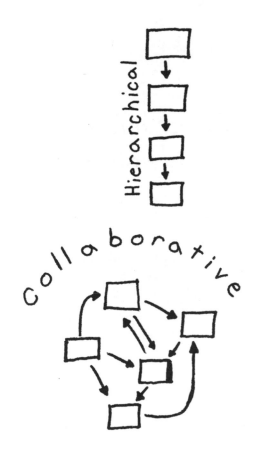

Great leaders
engage all three

Ways To See

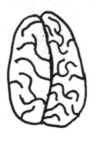

(Use All Three)

Keep the big picture in focus

Encourage cross-department inter-action

"The whole is greater than the sum of it's parts."

Make it easy for people to communicate internally.

Be open about challenges, plans, profits, wins, losses, and more.

FOUR BLIND GUYS
describe an elephant

Get the facts

Discuss   outcomes
           pitfalls
           options

Decide

3D's

of Decision Making

DATA

DIALOGUE

DECISION

THE AUTHOR
L and Artist

Daren Martin is a thought leader and organizational change agent who transforms companies. He has a PhD in psychology and years of experience leading change initiatives, architecting company cultures, and reinventing corporations. As a keynote speaker and teacher, Dr. Martin engages audiences across the world. His travels have taken him to over forty countries working with small, mid-sized, and Fortune 500 companies. He is an inspirational resource for business managers and collaborative teams. Daren resides in Dallas, Texas.

To submit and share your own
Whiteboard Business Model
go to...

WWW. Whiteboard Models. com

(You could be included in a)
(Future book!)